Twenty to Ma...

Knitted
Mug Hugs

Val Pierce

Search Press

First published in Great Britain 2010

Search Press Limited
Wellwood, North Farm Road,
Tunbridge Wells, Kent TN2 3DR

Reprinted 2011

Text copyright © Val Pierce 2010

Photographs by Debbie Patterson at
Search Press Studios

Photographs and design copyright
© Search Press Ltd 2010

ISBN: 978-1-84448-606-9

Suppliers
If you have difficulty in obtaining any of the
materials and equipment mentioned in this book,
then please visit the Search Press website for
details of suppliers: www.searchpress.com

Printed in Malaysia

Dedication
To Ellie, Abi and Oliver, three very special
little people. A true source of my inspiration
for all things bright and beautiful!

Safety note
Please ensure you wrap your mug cosy
around your mug or cup and secure it
before filling the mug or cup with hot liquid,
otherwise you may accidentally spill your
drink. Once filled, the mug or cup should be
held by the handle when in use to avoid it
slipping through your fingers and the drink
being spilt.

Contents

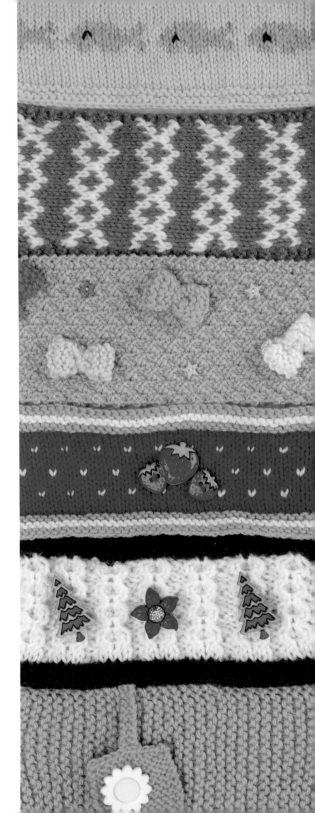

Introduction

Drinking a cup of tea or coffee will never be the same again with these fun and colourful mug hugs! What better way to keep your hot drinks hot than to create your own special cosy. In this little book I have designed twenty unique projects, each with an alternative colourway, in a range of colours and styles.

The patterns are easy to follow and the cosies quick to make, so they are ideal projects for those of you who are new to knitting, as well as more experienced knitters looking for something a little different to make for themselves, their family or their friends. They can be knitted up in just a few hours, and each project takes only a small amount of yarn, so they are ideal for using up all those odds and ends that you have stashed away.

Make a matching set of mug hugs to complement your favourite tea or coffee cups; make a personalised one for a special friend or close relative; create a set of mug hugs to celebrate Christmas, a birthday or a special occasion; make one for all the members of your work team, club or circle of friends; or simply treat yourself to your own special mug hug.

Whatever you decide to do, I hope that the designs in this book will inspire you all to 'get hugging'.

Happy knitting!

Decorative and useful, mug hugs will warm your heart as well as your drink. Here are just some of the designs featured in the book.

Hints and tips

There are no specific tensions set for any of the projects in the book, but if you decide to use different yarns from those stated do note that the mug cosy may turn out a little larger or smaller than the pattern states.

When a pattern is knitted lengthways it is possible to adjust the length by simply knitting more or fewer rows before completing the buttonhole band.

Fair Isle and stocking stitch tend to curl a little at the edges after they are knitted. Pressing the piece with a warm iron over a damp cloth can help to alleviate this and even out the patterning.

Abbreviations

The list of abbreviations shown opposite are the most common ones used in the book. Where abbreviations are used in one pattern only, they are given with the appropriate pattern for ease of reference.

UK and US terminology

UK	US
cast off	bind off
moss stitch	seed stitch
stocking stitch	stockinette stitch
yarn forward	yarn over

Button sizes

All the mug hugs in this book are designed to take a button that measures approximately 1.5–2.0cm (½–¾in) across.

The design shown opposite is given on page 36. The mug hug itself is knitted following the same pattern as that given for the project, but with the addition of the rose motif in place of the sheep. The instructions for the rose are given on page 37.

alt:	alternate
cm:	centimetres
dec:	decrease
GS:	garter stitch (every row knit)
inc:	increase
K:	knit
P:	purl
psso:	pass slipped stitch over
rem:	remaining
rep:	repeat
RS:	right side
skpo:	slip 1, knit 1, pass slipped stitch over
SS:	stocking stitch
st:	stitch
tog:	together
WS:	wrong side
yfwd:	bring yarn forward to increase 1 stitch
yrn:	yarn round needle (yfwd then go round the needle again)

Snowflakes and Stars

Materials:

1 ball dark blue double knitting yarn

7 white snowflake buttons

1 plain blue button

Needles:

1 pair 4.00mm (UK 8; US 6) knitting needles

Instructions:

Cast on 7 sts.

Knit 2 rows.

Continue in GS.

Inc 1 st at each end of next and every alt row until 19 sts on needle.

Proceed in GS and block pattern as follows:

Row 1: knit.

Row 2: K3, P6, K to end.

Rows 3–8: rep rows 1 and 2 three times.

Rows 9–11: knit.

Row 12: knit to last 9 sts, P6, K3.

Rows 13–18: rep rows 11 and 12, 3 times.

Row 19–20: knit.

Rep rows 1–20 twice, then rep rows 1–10 once.

Continue in GS and shape buttonhole end:

Dec 1 st at each end of next and every alt row until 11 sts on needle.

Next row: to make buttonhole, K2tog, K3, yrn, K2tog, knit to last 2 sts, K2tog.

Next row: knit, knitting into yrn of previous row.

Continue to dec as before until 7 sts rem.

Knit 2 rows.

Cast off.

To make up:

Work in all ends neatly. Sew the snowflake buttons into the squares, as shown in the photograph below. Sew the blue button on to the end of the mug hug to correspond with the buttonhole at the other end.

Measurements:

23 x 8cm (9 x 3¼in)

I knitted a smaller version, measuring 20 x 7cm (7¾ x 2¾in), by following the same pattern but using red, 4-ply yarn and size 3.25mm (UK 10; US 3) needles. I stitched a gold star button into the centre of each square.

Cosy Christmas

Materials:

1 ball cream double knitting yarn

Oddment of dark green double knitting yarn for edging

2 Christmas tree buttons

1 poinsettia button

1 green heart-shaped button

Needles:

1 pair 4.00mm (UK 8; US 6) knitting needles

Abbreviations:

tw2f work two stitches as follows: knit into front of second stitch, but do not slip stitch off needle. Now knit into first stitch in the normal way and slip both stitches off needle.

tw2b work two stitches as follows: knit into back of second stitch, but do not slip stitch off needle. Now knit into first stitch in the normal way and slip both stitches off the needle.

Instructions:

Using green yarn, cast on 44 sts.
Work 3 rows in GS.
Break yarn and join in cream.
Proceed in main pattern as follows:
Row 1 (RS facing): K2, (tw2f, tw2b, P2) 6 times, tw2f, tw2b, K2.
Row 2: K2, (P4, K2) to end of row.
Row 3: K2, (tw2b, tw2f, P2) 6 times, tw2b, tw2f, K2.
Row 4: as row 2.
Rep rows 1–4 three times.
Change to green yarn and work 4 rows in GS.
Cast off.

Button and buttonhole edges:

With RS facing and using green yarn, pick up and knit 17 sts evenly along one short edge of the mug cosy.
Knit 1 row.
Continue in GS.

Dec 1 st at each end of next and every alt row until 7 sts rem. Cast off.
Work along the other short edge in the same way, decreasing until 13 sts rem.
For the buttonhole, K2tog, K3, yrn twice, K2tog, K2, K2tog.
Next row: knit, dropping the extra loops of the previous row.
Continue to dec as before until 7 sts rem.
Cast off.

To make up:

Work in all ends neatly. Sew on the heart-shaped button to correspond with the buttonhole at the other end. Sew the poinsettia and Christmas tree buttons in position on the front of the mug hug.

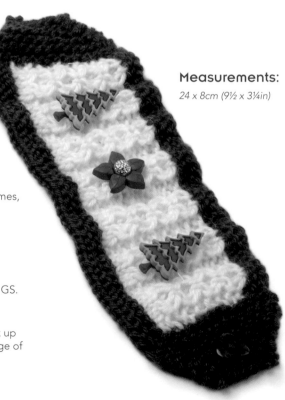

Measurements:

24 x 8cm (9½ x 3¼in)

For a seasonal touch, I have worked a red and white mug hug using the same pattern. Why not make a complete set in festive colours to adorn your favourite mugs at Christmas?

11

Leaf Fall

Materials:

1 ball beige double knitting yarn

Oddments of double knitting yarn in three shades of brown for leaves

3 ladybird buttons

1 flower button

Needles:

1 pair 4.00mm (UK 8; US 6) and 1 pair 3.25mm (UK 10; US 3) knitting needles

Abbreviations:

m1 make 1 st by picking up the horizontal loop that lies between the st you have just worked and the next st, then knit into the back of it.

Instructions:

Using 4.00mm (UK 8; US 6) needles and beige yarn, cast on 8 sts.
Continue in GS.
Knit 2 rows.
Inc 1 st at each end of next and every alt row until 18 sts on needle.
Commence pattern as follows:
Row 1: (K2, P2) to last 2 sts, K2.
Row 2: (P2, K2) to last 2 sts, P2.
Row 3: (P2, K2) to last 2 sts, P2.
Row 4: (K2, P2) to last 2 sts, K2.
Rep rows 1–4 to form pattern.
When work measures 19cm (7½in), continue in GS and work buttonhole band as follows:
Knit 2 rows in GS.
Dec 1 st at each end of next and every alt row until 12 sts rem.
Next row: K2tog, K3, yrn twice, K2tog, knit to last 2 sts, K2tog.
Next row: knit, dropping the yrn of the previous row and knitting into the loop.
Continue to dec as before until 8 sts rem.
Cast off.

Leaves:
(Make three, each in a different colour)

Using 3.25mm (UK 10; US 3) needles, cast on 5 sts.
Knit 2 rows in GS.
Shape as follows:
Row 1: K2, m1, K1, m1, K2 [7 sts].
Row 2: K3, P1, K3.
Row 3: K3, m1, K1, m1, K3 [9 sts].
Row 4: K4, P1, K4.
Row 5: knit.
Rep rows 4 and 5 twice.
Dec 1 st at each end of next and every following row until 3 sts rem.
Next row: K3tog, fasten off.

Measurements:

24 x 8cm (9½ x 3¼in)

To make up:
Work in all ends neatly. Embroider the veins on to the leaves, if desired, using chain stitch. Position the leaves in the centre of the mug cosy, overlapping them slightly. Sew in place then stitch a ladybird button in the centre of the leaves and on either end of the cosy. Sew on the flower button to correspond with the buttonhole.

Keep your hot soup hot on chilly autumnal days with this pair of seasonal mug hugs. The alternative version has been knitted using brown wool, and decorated with green leaves.

Butterflies and Beads

Materials:

1 ball lilac 4-ply yarn
120 silver embroidery beads, size 7
1 embroidered butterfly motif
1 lilac heart-shaped button

Needles:

1 pair 3.25mm (UK 10; US 3) knitting needles

Instructions:

Cast on 52 sts.
Knit 4 rows in GS.
Knit next 2 rows in SS.
Begin lacy pattern as follows:
Row 1: K1, *K2tog, yfwd, K1, yfwd, skpo*, rep
from * to * to last st, K1.
Row 2: purl.
Rep rows 1 and 2 eight times.
Knit 2 rows in SS.
Knit 4 rows in GS. Cast off.

Button edge:

With RS facing, pick up and knit 21 sts evenly
along one short edge.
Continue in GS.
Dec 1 st at each end of next and every alt row
until 9 sts rem. Cast off.

Buttonhole edge:

Work as for button edge until 15 sts rem.
Next row: for the buttonhole, K2tog, K5, yrn
twice, K2tog, knit to last 2 sts, K2tog.
Next row: knit, dropping the yrn of the previous
row and knitting into the loops.
Continue to dec as before until 9 sts rem.
Cast off.

To make up:

Work in all ends neatly. Sew the beads on to
the long edges of the mug hug. Place one
bead on every other stitch in the first row, then
place them in between these in the second
row. Sew the embroidered butterfly motif to
the buttonhole end of the mug hug. At the
other end sew on the heart-shaped button to
correspond with the buttonhole.

Measurements:

23 x 8cm (9 x 3¼in)

*In pink or lilac, these
pretty mug hugs add a
touch of feminine charm
to your evening drink.*

Buttons and Bows

Materials:

1 ball lilac 4-ply yarn

Oddments of 4-ply yarn in four different colours for bows

4 mini star buttons

1 purple flower button

Needles:

1 pair 3.25mm (UK 10; US 3) knitting needles

Instructions:

Cast on 10 sts using lilac yarn.
Knit 2 rows. Continue in GS.
Inc 1 st at each end of next and every alt row until 22 sts on needle.
Commence pattern as follows:
Row 1: (K2, P2) to last 2 sts, K2.
Row 2: (P2, K2) to last 2 sts, P2.
Row 3: (P2, K2) to last 2 sts, P2.

Row 4: (K2, P2) to last 2 sts K2.
Rep rows 1–4 to form pattern.
When work measures 19cm (7½in), change to GS and work buttonhole band as follows:
Knit 2 rows in GS.
Dec 1 st at each end of next and every alt row until 16 sts rem.
Next row: for buttonhole, K2tog, K5, yrn twice, K2tog, knit to last 2 sts, K2tog.
Next row: knit, dropping the yrn of the previous row and knitting into the loops.
Continue to dec as before until 10 sts rem.
Cast off.

Bows:

(Make four, each in a different colour)
Cast on 5 sts.
Work 32 rows in GS. Cast off.

To make up:

Work in all ends neatly. To make each bow, fold a strip of knitting in half and join neatly along the short edges. Re-fold the work so that the join is at the centre back of the strip. Take a sewing needle and matching yarn, and run the yarn through the centre of the strip from side to side. Gather up the knitting to form the bow. You may need to run the yarn back and forth several times to achieve a good shape. Secure the yarn at the back. Stitch all the bows randomly on to the front of the mug cosy. Now sew on the mini star buttons in between the bows. Take the flower button and stitch it on one end of the mug hug to correspond with the buttonhole at the other.

Measurements:

23 x 8cm (9 x 3¼in)

These pretty mug hugs work well in pastel colours, and make ideal gifts for anyone with a sweet nature!

Cat's Whiskers

Materials:

1 ball gold-coloured 4-ply yarn

Oddments of 4-ply yarn in black, white and pale pink

2 small green beads

1 yellow flower button

tiny piece of stuffing

Needles:

1 pair 3.25mm (UK 10; US 3) knitting needles

Measurements:

22 x 8cm (8¾ x 3¼in)

Instructions:

Using gold-coloured yarn, cast on 8 sts.

Knit 2 rows.

Continue in GS.

Inc 1 st at each end of next and every alt row until 20 sts on needle.

Commence pattern as follows:

Row 1: (K4, P4) twice, K4.

Row 2: (P4, K4) twice, P4.

Row 3: (P4, K4) twice, P4.

Row 4: (K4, P4) twice, K4.

Rep rows 1–4 until work measures 18cm (7in) ending on either row 2 or row 4.

Change to GS.

Knit 1 row.

Dec 1 st at each end of next and every alt row until 14 sts rem.

Next row: to make buttonhole, K2tog, K4, yrn twice, K4, K2tog.

Next row: knit, dropping the yrn of the previous row and knitting into the loops.

Continue to dec as before until 8 sts rem.

Knit 2 rows. Cast off.

Cat's head:

Using black yarn, cast on 6 sts.

Working in SS, inc 1 st at each end of every row until 14 sts on needle.

Work 4 rows, ending with a purl row.

Dec 1 st at each end of every row until 8 sts rem, ending with a purl row. Cast off.

Ears:

(Make two)

Using black yarn, cast on 7 sts.

Work 4 rows in GS.

Dec 1 st at each end of every row until 3 sts rem.

K3tog, fasten off.

Nose:

Using white yarn, cast on 6 sts.

Working in GS, knit 2 rows.

Inc 1 st at each end of next and every alt row until 10 sts on needle.

Knit 2 rows.

Dec 1 st at each end of every row until 2 sts rem.

Knit 2 rows on these sts.

K2tog, fasten off.

To make up:

Work in all ends neatly. To make the cat's head and face, place the nose section on to the head and sew it in place, adding a tiny piece of stuffing to fill out the nose. Sew the ears to the head. Using black yarn, embroider the nose and mouth. Thread black yarn through the nose section to represent whiskers. Embroider tiny triangles inside each ear using pink yarn and sew on green beads for the eyes. Stitch the finished head to the centre of the mug cosy. Sew on the yellow flower button to correspond with the buttonhole.

Animal lovers will adore these brightly coloured mug hugs. Try altering the colours to match your own pet, or with only slight changes to the pattern you could try knitting a mouse, rabbit or dog on the mug hug instead!

Celtic Plait

Materials:
1 ball leaf-green double knitting yarn

1 green flower button

Needles:
1 pair 4.00mm (UK 8; US 6) and 1 pair 3.25mm (UK 10; US 3) knitting needles

1 cable needle

Abbreviations:
CB3 slip next 3 sts on to cable needle and leave at back of work. Knit next 3 sts, then knit 3 sts from cable needle.

CF3 slip next 3 sts on to cable needle and leave at front of work. Knit next 3 sts, then knit 3 sts from cable needle.

Instructions:
Using 4.00mm (UK 8; US 6) needles and green yarn, cast on 26 sts.
Commence cable pattern as follows:
Row 1: K1, P3, K18, P3, K1.
Row 2: K4, P18, K4.
Row 3: K1, P3, (CB3) 3 times, P3, K1.
Row 4: K4, P18, K4.
Row 5: K1, P3, K18, P3, K1.
Row 6: K4, P18, K4.
Row 7: K1, P3, K3, (CF3) twice, K3, P3, K1.
Row 8: K4, P18, K4.
Continue in pattern until work measures 23cm (9in) ending on either row 3 or row 7.
Change to 3.25mm (UK 10; US 3) needles and dec 7 sts evenly across row [19 sts].
Working in GS, dec 1 st at each end of next and every alt row until 9 sts rem.
Cast off.

Using 3.25mm (UK 10; US 3) needles, pick up and knit 19 sts along the other short edge.
Knit 1 row.
Continue in GS.
Dec 1 st at each end of next and every alt row until 13 sts rem.
Next row: to make buttonhole, K2tog, K4, yrn twice, K2tog, K3, K2tog.
Next row: knit, dropping the yrn of the previous row and knitting into the loops.
Continue to dec as before until 9 sts rem.
Cast off.

To make up:
Work in all ends neatly. Attach the green flower button to correspond to the buttonhole at the other end.

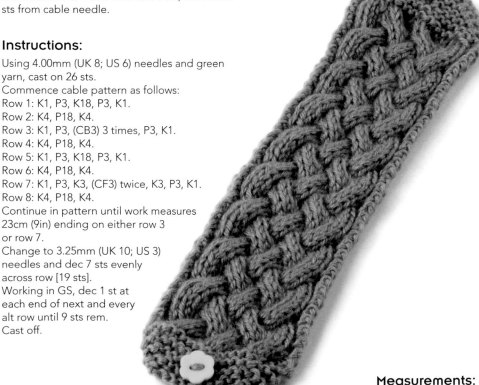

Measurements:
25 x 6cm (9¾ x 2¼in)

Perfect for cosy nights in front of the fire, these chunky mug hugs will surely appeal to the man in your life!

Cottage Garden

Materials:

1 ball green double knitting yarn

1 ball blue double knitting yarn

Oddments of double knitting yarn in various colours for embroidering the flowers

3 bee buttons

1 flower button

Needles:

1 pair 4.00mm (UK 8; US 6) knitting needles

Measurements:

25 x 8cm (9¾ x 3¼in)

Instructions:

Using green double knitting yarn, cast on 43 sts. Work 12 rows in GS.

Change to blue yarn and proceed in moss stitch (US seed stitch) for 10 rows.

Change to GS and work 4 rows. Cast off.

Button edge:

With RS facing and using blue yarn, pick up and knit 17 sts evenly along one short edge.

Knit 1 row. Continue in GS.

Dec 1 st at each end of next and every alt row until 7 sts rem. Cast off.

Buttonhole edge:

Work other short edge in same way until 13 sts rem.

Next row: to make buttonhole, K2tog, K3, yrn twice, K2tog, K2, K2tog.

Next row: knit, dropping the yrn of the previous row and knitting into the loops.

Continue to dec as before until 7 sts rem. Cast off.

To make up:

Embroider the flower stems on to the mug cosy using green yarn and stem stitch. Add tiny flowers on the top and sides of each stem using French knots. Sew the bee buttons on to the flowers and add the flower button at the opposite end to the buttonhole.

This alternative design has been decorated with four colourful flowers. Work the stems and leaves in chain stitch, and then sew a flower button on to the top of each stem. These pretty mug hugs are perfect for keeping your drink hot during a well-deserved rest from tending the garden!

23

Fair Isle Hearts

Materials:

1 ball dusty pink double knitting yarn
1 ball light blue double knitting yarn
1 fancy matching button

Needles:

1 pair 4.00mm (UK 8; US 6) knitting needles

Instructions:

Using pink yarn, cast on 53 sts.
Work 4 rows in GS.
Join in blue yarn and knit 2 rows in SS.
Join in pink yarn and work 9 rows in
Fair Isle pattern, working from the
chart. Read right-side rows from
right to left and strand yarn not in
use loosely across back of work.
Pulling the yarn too tightly will
cause the work to pucker.
When Fair Isle pattern is complete,
continue in blue yarn as follows:
Next row: purl.
Work 2 rows in SS.
Join in pink yarn and work 4 rows in GS.
Cast off.

Button and buttonhole edges:

With RS facing and using pink yarn, pick up and
knit 17 sts evenly along one short edge.
Knit 1 row.
Working in GS, dec 1 st at each of next and
every alt row until 7 sts rem.
Cast off.
Work along other short edge in same way until
11 sts rem.

Measurements:

25 x 7cm (9¾ x 2¾in)

Next row: to make the buttonhole, K2tog, K3,
yrn twice, K2tog, K2, K2tog.
Next row: knit, dropping the yrn of the previous
row and knitting into the loops.
Continue to dec as before until 7 sts rem.
Cast off.

To make up:

Work in all ends neatly and then sew on the
button to correspond with the buttonhole at
the other end.

Colour chart

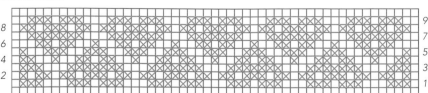

These stylish mug hugs work well in a variety of colourways. Why not make a cosy pair for you and your loved one!

Coffee and Cream

Materials:
1 ball coffee-coloured double knitting yarn

Oddment of cream textured yarn

1 wooden button

Needles:
1 pair 4.00mm (UK 8; US 6) knitting needles

Instructions:
Cast on 44 sts.
Proceed in pattern as follows:
Row 1: (RS facing) knit.
Row 2: purl.
Row 3: knit.
Row 4: knit.
Row 5: purl.
Row 6: knit.
Rep rows 1–6 three times.
Change to cream textured yarn and work 8 rows in GS. Cast off.

Button edge:
With RS facing and coffee-coloured yarn, pick up and knit 17 sts evenly along one short edge.
Knit 1 row.
Continue in GS.
Dec 1 st at each end of next and every alt row until 7 sts rem. Cast off.

Buttonhole edge:
Work along the other short edge in the same way until 11 sts rem.
Next row: to make buttonhole, K2tog, K3, yrn twice, K2tog, K2, K2tog.
Next row: knit, dropping the yrn of the previous row and knitting into the loops.

Continue to dec as before until 7 sts rem. Cast off.

To make up:
Work in all ends neatly. Sew on the wooden button to correspond with the buttonhole at the other end.

Measurements:
26 x 8cm (10¼ x 3¼in)

Add a touch of luxury to your creamy coffee with these sumptuous cosies. The alternative version is worked in black.

Highland Hugs

Materials:

1 ball blue double knitting yarn

1 ball lilac double knitting yarn

1 blue cross-shaped button

Needles:

1 pair 3.75mm (UK 9; US 5) knitting needles

Instructions:

Using lilac yarn, cast on 9 sts.
Knit 1 row.
Continue in GS.
Inc 1 st at each end of next and every
alt row until 21 sts on needle.
Next row: knit.
Next row: K2, purl to last 2 sts, K2.
Rep last 2 rows once.
Join in blue yarn and work Fair Isle pattern from
chart, as follows, starting with RS facing:

*Row 1: K2 lilac, (row 1 of chart), K2 lilac.
Row 2: P2 lilac (row 2 of chart), P2 lilac.
Rep for rows 3–7, beginning and ending each
row with K2 or P2 lilac. Read right-side rows
from right to left, and yarn not in use should be
stranded loosely across back of work. Do not
pull the yarn too tightly as this will cause the
work to pucker.
Beginning with a purl row, work 3 rows in SS
using lilac yarn only. *
Rep from * to * 4 times.
Break off blue yarn and continue in GS and lilac
yarn only.
Dec 1 st at each end of next and every alt row
until 13 sts rem.
Next row: to make buttonhole, K2tog, K4, yrn,
K2tog, knit to last 2 sts, K2tog.
Next row: knit, knitting into the yrn of the
previous row.
Continue to dec as before until 9 sts rem.
Cast off.

To make up:

Work in all ends neatly. Sew on the button
to correspond with the buttonhole. Press the
piece lightly with a warm iron over a damp cloth
to even the pattern.

Colour chart

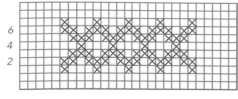

28

Hot coffee and marshmallows, wrapped in stylish mug hugs – how better to end a brisk walk in the countryside or a day on the ski slopes!

Gold Fish

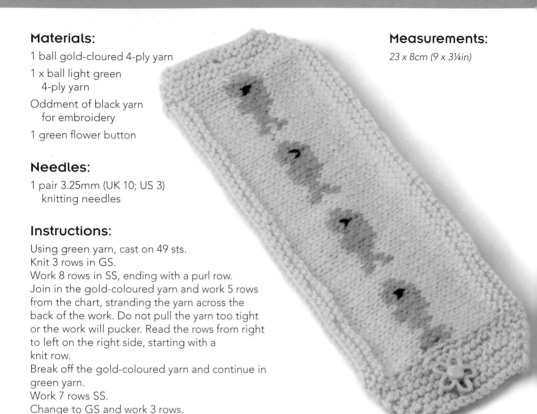

Materials:

1 ball gold-cloured 4-ply yarn

1 x ball light green
4-ply yarn

Oddment of black yarn
for embroidery

1 green flower button

Needles:

1 pair 3.25mm (UK 10; US 3)
knitting needles

Instructions:

Using green yarn, cast on 49 sts.
Knit 3 rows in GS.
Work 8 rows in SS, ending with a purl row.
Join in the gold-coloured yarn and work 5 rows from the chart, stranding the yarn across the back of the work. Do not pull the yarn too tight or the work will pucker. Read the rows from right to left on the right side, starting with a knit row.
Break off the gold-coloured yarn and continue in green yarn.
Work 7 rows SS.
Change to GS and work 3 rows.
Cast off.

Button edge:

With RS facing, and using green yarn, pick up and knit 21 sts along one short edge.
Knit 1 row.
Continue in GS and dec 1 st at each end of next and every alt row until 15 sts rem. Cast off.

Buttonhole edge:

Work as button edge until 19 sts rem.
Next row: to make buttonhole, K2tog, K7, yrn twice, K2tog, knit to last 2 sts, K2tog.

Measurements:

23 x 8cm (9 x 3¼in)

Next row: knit, dropping the yrn of the previous row and knitting into the loops.
Continue to dec as before until 15 sts rem.
Cast off.

To make up:

Work in all ends neatly. Embroider an eye in black on each of the fish. Sew the button on to correspond with the buttonhole at the other end.

Colour chart

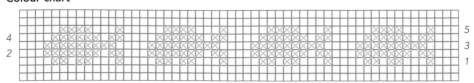

These gorgeous mug hugs suit any occasion, but are perfect for enjoying a hot drink outdoors. Why not make a set in your favourite colours and keep them in the picnic basket.

Lady's Smock

Materials:

1 ball pink double knitting yarn

20 gold-coloured glass beads

1 fancy pink button

Needles:

1 pair 3.75mm (UK 9; US 5) knitting needles

Blunt-ended sewing needle for smocking

Instructions:

Cast on 11 sts.

Knit 2 rows.

Continue in GS.

Inc 1 st at each end of next and every alt row until 23 sts on needle.

Proceed in pattern as follows:

Row 1: (RS facing) K2 ,(P3, K1) 4 times, P3, K2.

Row 2: K2, (K3, P1) 4 times, K3, K2.

Rep rows 1 and 2 until work measures 18cm (7in), ending on row 2.

Change to GS and shape the button edge as follows:

Dec 1 st at each end of next and every alt row until 17 sts rem.

Next row: to make buttonhole, K2tog, K6, yrn, K2tog, knit to last 2 sts, K2tog.

Next row: knit, knitting into the yrn of the previous row.

Continue shaping as before until 11 sts rem.

Knit 2 rows.

Cast off.

To make up and smock:

Work in all ends neatly. You will need to count your rows and divide them equally into sections. There should be 5 diamond shapes going down the centre of the design and 6 on either side. With RS facing and using a blunt-ended needle and pink yarn, catch together the lines of knit stitches to form the diamond shapes. Begin at the top of the piece of work and draw together the stitches in the two left-hand lines first, then those in the two right-hand lines, and finally the two inner lines. Stitch a bead on to each intersection. Follow the picture for guidance. Sew on the pink button to correspond with the buttonhole.

Measurements:

23 x 8cm (9 x 3¼in)

Give traditional
English afternoon tea a
contemporary twist with
these pretty mug hugs,
knitted in any colours
you choose.

Rambling Rose

Materials:

1 ball cherry red 4-ply yarn

Oddments of pink and green 4-ply yarn

1 red button

Needles:

1 pair 3.25mm (UK 10; US 3) knitting needles

2 double-pointed 3.25mm
(UK 10; US 3) needles

Instructions:

Using red yarn, cast on 15 sts.

Work in moss stitch (US seed stitch) for 7cm
(2¾in).Cast off.

Button edge:

With RS facing and using red yarn, pick
up and knit 21 sts evenly along one
short edge.

Continue in GS.

Dec 1 st at each end of next and every
alt row until 9 sts rem. Cast off.

Buttonhole edge:

Work as for button edge until 15 sts rem.

Next row: to make buttonhole, K2tog,
K5, yrn twice, K2tog, K to last 2 sts, K2tog.

Next row: knit, dropping the yrn of previous
row and knitting into the loops.

Continue to dec as before until 9 sts rem.
Cast off.

Roses:

(Make three)

Using pink yarn, cast on 8 sts.

Next row: purl.

Next row: inc knitwise in each st to end [16 sts].

Next row: cast off first st in normal way,*yrn,
pass st on needle over the yrn, cast off next st
in the normal way*. Rep from * to * until all sts
are cast off.

The work will curl as you cast off. Coil it into a
rose shape and secure with a few stitches.

Leaves:

(Make three)

Using green yarn, cast on 3 sts.

Rows 1–2: knit. Continue in GS.

Rows 3–5: inc 1 st at each end of row on next
and every alt row until 7 sts on needle.

Rows 6–7: knit.

Row 8: K2tog at each end [5 sts].

Row 9: K1, sl1, K2tog, psso, K1.

Row 10: K1, K2tog.

Row 11: K2tog.

Fasten off.

Stems:

Make an i-cord for the rose stems.

Using green yarn and the double-pointed
needles, cast on 3 sts.

Knit the first row.

Slide the sts to the opposite end of the needle.
The working yarn is at the end of the row. With
the same side facing you, knit the next row,

Measurements:

24 x 7cm (9½ x 2¾in)

pulling the working yarn up taut at the back of the piece so you can knit with it. Again, slide the sts to the opposite end of the needle. Continue in this way, always keeping the RS of the work facing you. As you pull the yarn, the back of the work will close up on itself, forming a neat tube. Continue until the piece measures approximately 24cm (9½in). Cast off.

To make up:
Work in all ends neatly. Arrange the i-cord stem on the mug cosy in a twisting shape and sew it in place with matching yarn. Arrange the roses and leaves along the stem and stitch in place. Sew on the button to correspond with the buttonhole at the other end.

This lovely design will make your favourite mugs even more eye-catching. Knit them in a range of colours to coordinate with your most treasured pieces.

Warm and Woolly

Materials:

1 ball blue 4-ply yarn
Oddment of black 4-ply yarn
Small amount of white bouclé yarn
1 blue flower button

Needles:

1 pair 3.25mm (UK 10; US 3) and 1 pair 3.75mm
   (UK 9; US 5) knitting needles

Instructions:

Using blue yarn and 3.25mm (UK 10, US 3)
needles, cast on 11 sts.
Knit 1 row.
Working in GS, inc 1 st at each end of next and
every alt row until 21 sts on needle.
Commence pattern as follows:
Row 1: knit.
Rows 2–3: purl.
Row 4: knit.
Rep rows 1–4 until work
measures 17cm (6¾in),
ending on row 4.
Change to GS and
shape end.
Dec 1 st at each end of
next and every alt row until
15 sts rem.
Next row: to make buttonhole,
K2tog, K5, yrn, K2tog, knit to
last 2 sts, K2tog.
Next row: knit, knitting into the yrn
of the previous row.
Continue in GS. Dec as before until
11 sts rem. Cast off.

Sheep's body:

Using bouclé yarn and 3.75mm (UK 9; US 5)
needles, cast on 8 sts.
Purl 1 row.
Next row: knit, inc 1 st at each end of row.
Work 5 rows in SS.
Dec 1 st at each end of next and every alt row
until 2 sts rem. Cast off.

Legs:

(Make two)
Using 3.25mm (UK 10; US 3) needles and black
yarn, cast on 8 sts.
Knit 1 row. Cast off.

Head:

Using 3.25mm (UK 10; US 3) needles and black
yarn, cast on 12 sts.
Working in GS, knit 2 rows.
Rows 3–4: cast off 3 sts at beg of row [6 sts].
Rows 5–8: knit.
Row 9: K2tog, K2, K2tog [4 sts].
Row 10: K2tog twice.
Row 11: K2tog. Fasten off.

To make up:

Work in all ends neatly. Place the sheep's body
on to the centre of the mug hug and stitch it in
place. Tuck the tops of the legs under the body
and secure. Attach the head to the body. Wind
a short length of bouclé yarn into a small coil
and sew it to the top of the sheep's head.
Sew on the button to correspond with
the buttonhole at the other end.

Measurements:

20 x 8cm (7¾ x 3¼in)
*Note: This pattern produces
very stretchy knitting, so
the mug hug can fit a
slightly larger mug
than the given
measurements.*

To make the rose on this glamorous alternative design:

Using size 3.25mm (UK 10; US 3) needles and pink yarn, cast on 12 sts.

Row 1: purl.
Row 2: K10, turn and purl to end.
Row 3: K8, turn and purl to end.
Row 4: K6, turn and purl to end.
Row 5: K4, turn and purl to end.
Row 6: K2, turn and purl to end.
Row 7: knit.
Row 8: purl.
Rep rows 2–8 ten more times. Cast off.
Make two leaves, worked in GS, as follows:

Using the same needles and green yarn, cast on 5 sts. Knit 1 row.

Inc 1 st at each end of next and every alt row until 11 sts on needle.
Knit 4 rows.
Dec 1 st at each end of every row until 3 sts rem. K3tog, fasten off.

To make up, coil the rose into a tight spiral and fold over the outer edges to form petals. Sew together at the join. Stitch a few glass beads on to the rose to form dew drops. Sew the leaves together and stitch them to the back of the rose. Sew the completed flower to the centre of a black mug hug. Sew on a black button to correspond with the buttonhole.

Time for Tea

Materials:

1 ball red double knitting yarn

Oddments of 4-ply yarn in pale turquoise and green

3 pink flower buttons

Needles:

1 pair 4.00mm (UK 8; US 6) and 1 pair 3.25mm (UK 10; US 3) knitting needles

Instructions:

Using 4.00mm (UK 8; US 6) needles and red yarn, cast on 7 sts.
Knit 2 rows. Continue in GS.
Inc 1 st at each end of next and every alt row until 17 sts on needle.
Work 64 rows in GS.
Dec 1 st at each end of next and every alt row until 11 sts rem.
Next row: to make the buttonhole, K2tog, K3, yrn twice, K2tog, K2, K2tog.
Next row: knit, dropping the yrn of previous row and knitting into the loops.
Continue to dec until 7 sts rem.
Work 2 rows in GS.
Cast off.

Tea bag:

Using 3.25mm (UK 10; US 3) needles and turquoise yarn, cast on 13 sts.
Work 22 rows in GS.
Next row: cast off 5 sts, knit to end.
Next row: cast off 5 sts, knit to end.
Work 6cm (2¼in) in GS on rem 3 sts. Cast off.

Leaf:

Using 3.25mm (UK 10; US 3) needles and green yarn, cast on 3 sts.
Knit 2 rows.
Inc 1 st at each end of next and every alt row until 7 sts on needle.
Work 2 rows in GS.
Next row: K2tog at each end of row.
Next row: K1, sl1, K2tog, psso, K1.
Next row: K1, K2tog.
Next row: K2tog. Fasten off.

To make up:

Work in all ends neatly. Sew two buttons and the leaf on to the centre of the tea bag. Attach the tea bag by stitching the top of the cord to the back of the mug cosy. Sew on the remaining button to correspond with the buttonhole.

Measurements:

21 x 8cm (8¼ x 3¼in)

Give these simple designs a personal touch to make a special gift for a friend or relative. For example, add buttons or motifs to the teabag that reflect their favourite colours, pets, hobbies or interests.

43

Sunflowers

Materials:

1 ball turquoise double knitting yarn

Oddments of yellow, green and black double knitting yarn

2 sunflower buttons

1 bee button

Needles:

1 pair 4.00mm (UK 8; US 6) and 1 pair 3.25mm (UK 10; US 3) knitting needles

2 double-pointed 3.25mm (UK 10; US 3) needles

Instructions:

Using 4.00mm (UK 8; US 6) and turquoise yarn, cast on 5 sts.

Knit 2 rows. Continue in GS.

Inc 1 st at each end of next and every alt row until 17 sts on needle.

Commence pattern as follows:

Row 1: knit.

Row 2: K5, P7, K5.

Rows 3–8: rep rows 1 and 2 three times.

Rows 9–14: work in GS.

Rep rows 1–14 three times.

Rep rows 1–8 once.

Continue in GS, shaping the end and making the buttonhole as follows:

Dec 1 st at each end of next and every alt row until 11 sts rem.

Next row: to make buttonhole, K2tog, K3, yrn twice, K2tog, K2, K2tog.

Next row: knit, dropping the yrn of the previous row and knitting into the loops.

Continue to dec as before until 5 sts rem.

Knit 2 rows.

Cast off.

Sunflowers:

(Make two flowers for each sunflower)

Using 3.25mm (UK 10; US 3) needles and yellow yarn, cast on 57 sts.

Commence pattern as follows:

Row 1: purl.

Row 2: K2, *K1, slip this st back on to left-hand needle, lift next 8 sts on left-hand needle over this st and off the needle, yrn twice, knit the first st again, K2*. Rep from * to *.

Row 3: K1, **P2tog, drop loop of previous row and (K1, K1tbl) into loop, P1**. Rep from ** to ** to last st, K1.

Do not cast off. Run yarn through rem sts, then draw up into a flower shape and secure.

Centre of flower:

Using 3.25mm (UK 10; US 3) needles and black yarn, cast on 4 sts.

Knit 1 row.

Next row: inc 1 st at each end of row [6 sts].

Work 4 rows in GS.

Dec 1 st at each end of next row.

Knit 1 row. Cast off.

Stem:

Using green yarn, make an i-cord, approximately 5cm (2in) long, following the instructions on page 34.

Measurements:

25 x 8cm (9¾ x 3¼in)

Leaves:
(Make two)

Using green yarn and 3.25mm (UK 10; US 3) needles, cast on 4 sts.

Commence pattern as follows:

Knit 2 rows.

Working in GS, inc 1 st at each end of next and every alt row until 10 sts on needle.

Work 4 rows in GS.

Dec 1 st at each end of next and every alt row until 2 sts rem.

K2tog and fasten off.

To make up:
Work in all ends neatly. Place the two flower pieces on top of each other, offsetting the petals slightly, and sew together. Stitch the centre into the flower. Sew the stem and leaves in place on the central square of the mug hug, then stitch the sunflower on top. Sew the sunflower buttons on to the end two squares. Sew on the bee button to correspond with the buttonhole.

These bright and sunny mug hugs have a country feel that will cheer up your tea or coffee break whatever the weather!

Candy Twist

Materials:

1 ball turquoise double knitting yarn

1 ball lilac double knitting yarn

1 blue flower button

Needles:

1 pair 4.00mm (UK 8; US 6) knitting needles

1 cable needle

Abbreviations:

C8F cable 8 front, worked over next 8 sts as follows: slip next 4 sts on to cable needle and leave at front of work, knit next 4 sts, knit 4 sts from cable needle.

C8B cable 8 back, worked over next 8 sts as follows: slip next 4 sts on to cable needle and leave at back of work, knit next 4 sts, knit 4 sts from cable needle.

Instructions:

Using turquoise yarn, cast on 8 sts.

Knit 2 rows.

Inc 1 st at each end of next and every alt row until 20 sts on needle.

Proceed with two-colour cable pattern as follows. You will need to use separate balls of turquoise yarn either side of the lilac cable, twisting the yarn together when changing colours to avoid any holes in the work.

Row 1: K6 turquoise, K8 lilac, K6 turquoise.

Row 2: K6 turquoise, P8 lilac, K6 turquoise.

Row 3: K6 turquoise, C8B lilac, K6 turquoise.

Row 4: K6 turquoise, P8 lilac, K6 turquoise.

Rows 5–10: rep rows 1 and 2 three times.

Rep rows 1–10 until work measures approximately 20cm (7¾in), ending with row 4. Break off lilac yarn and continue in turquoise yarn and GS.

Dec 1 st at each end of next and every alt row until 14 sts rem.

Next row: to make the buttonhole, K2tog, K4, yrn, K2tog, knit to last 2 sts, K2tog.

Next row: knit, knitting into the yrn of the previous row.

Continue to dec as before until 8 sts rem.

Knit 2 rows. Cast off.

To make up:

Work in all ends neatly and sew on the button to correspond with the buttonhole.

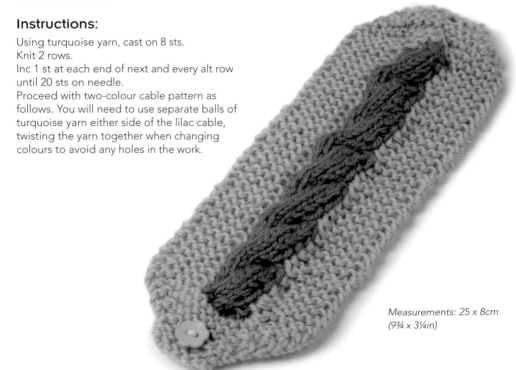

Measurements: 25 x 8cm (9¾ x 3¼in)

Work the pink and yellow version of this design in the same way, substituting C8F for C8B in row 3 of the pattern.

Acknowledgements
Many thanks to my family and friends for all their encouragement and patience whilst I was making this book. Thank you also to Coats Patons and Cygnet yarns for providing some of the yarns needed to make the projects, and last but not least a big thank you to all at Search Press for the wonderful job they have done in producing such a beautiful little book.